Made in the USA
Monee, IL
05 March 2023

29229699R00070